D0241772

My First Orchestra Book

Published by Naxos Books,
an imprint of Naxos Rights US, Inc.

www.naxosbooks.com

Printed and bound in China by L.Rex
Design and layout: Hannah Whale, Fruition – Creative Concepts
Sound editor: Sarah Butcher

A CIP Record for this book is available from the British Library.

ISBN: 978-1-84379-770-8

Contents

This is Tormod
the Troll.

He lives at the top of a
snowy mountain in Norway.

Tormod loves music!

But there is only one piece of music to listen to on his mountain. So...

...he ran away.

He wanted to discover MORE music!

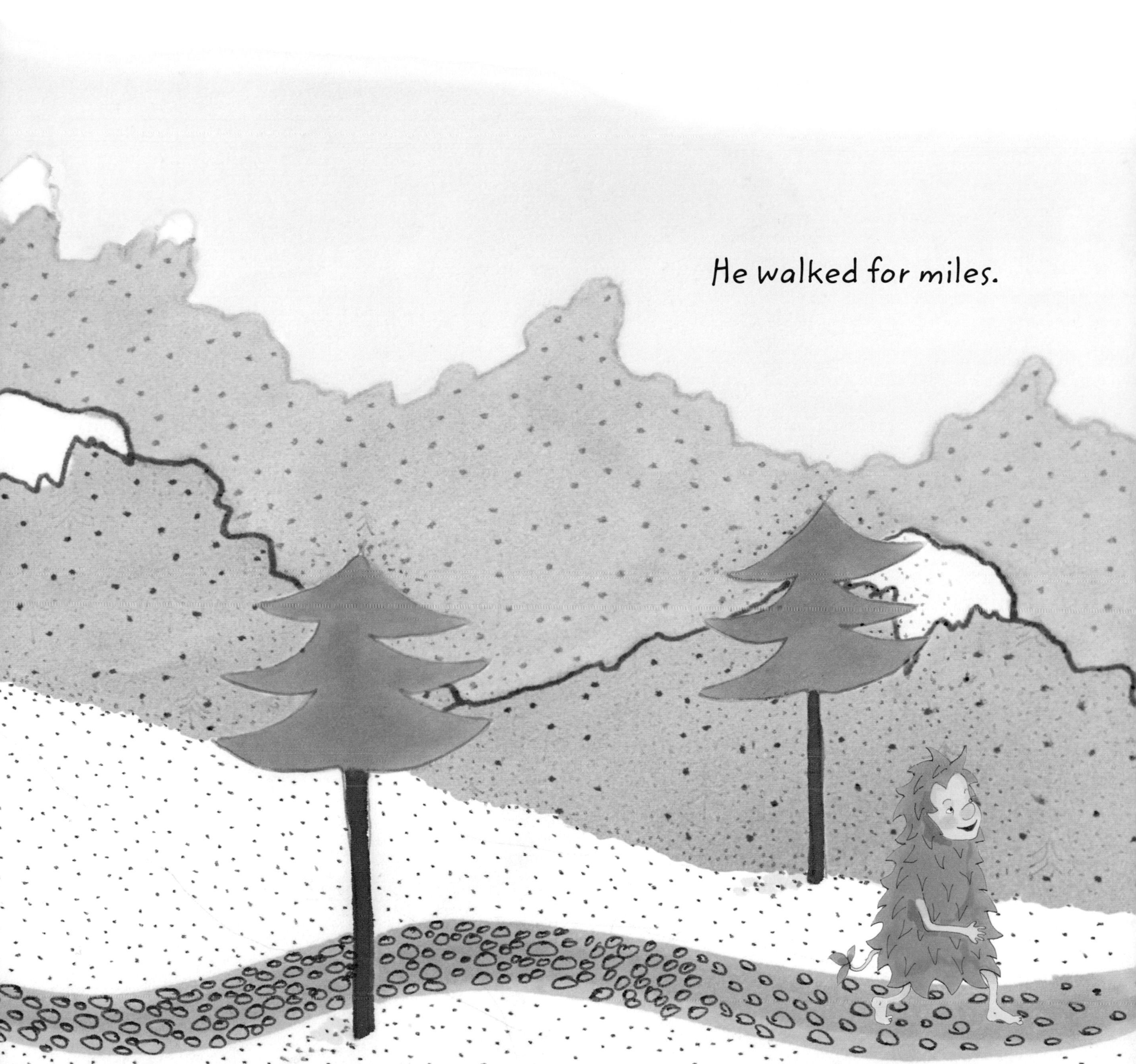

He walked for miles.

He found real people,
like you!

And then, he found
something amazing...

An orchestra!

Tormod was so excited!

But now he wants to go home and tell the other trolls about it, and he can't: he's stuck in the orchestra.

To get home, he needs to find his favourite music – the piece that they play on his mountain.

The Orchestra
Travel with Tormod
through the orchestra while
he looks for his music.
Listen
Play the CD
tracks marked
on each page
until you find again the
music you heard
on track 1.

The Orchestra

This is the whole orchestra together! It's a team – the biggest and most important team in music!

Listen 2

Full Orchestra

This is the beginning of Mozart's famous opera *The Magic Flute*, before the curtain goes up.
Wolfgang Amadeus **Mozart**
The Magic Flute
Overture (extract)

Listen 3

Full Orchestra

Ready... steady... go! Lively dance music from Tchaikovsky's ballet *The Nutcracker.*

Pyotr Il'yich **Tchaikovsky**
The Nutcracker
Russian Dance

Families

Did you know that instruments are grouped into 'families'?

Does your family have big people and small people? People with low voices and people with high voices?

Well, each family in the orchestra is like that too: it has big instruments (which are low-sounding) and small instruments (which are high-sounding).

But in every family, the people or instruments are related to each other. They have things in common. Often they look similar.

Strings

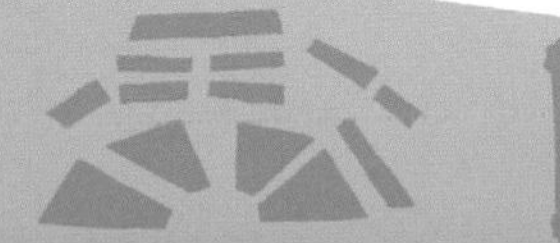

These are the
main families in
the orchestra.
Brass
Woodwind
Percussion

String Family

Violins Violas Cellos Double Basses

This is the biggest family in the orchestra. The instruments all look alike but they are different sizes. Each is made of top-quality wood and has four strings.

horse hair

tip

wooden stick

frog

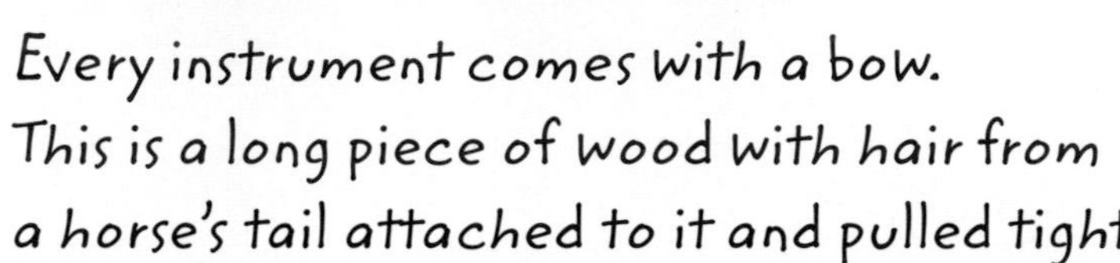

Every instrument comes with a bow. This is a long piece of wood with hair from a horse's tail attached to it and pulled tight.

When the hair of the bow is dragged across the strings, the instrument makes a sound.

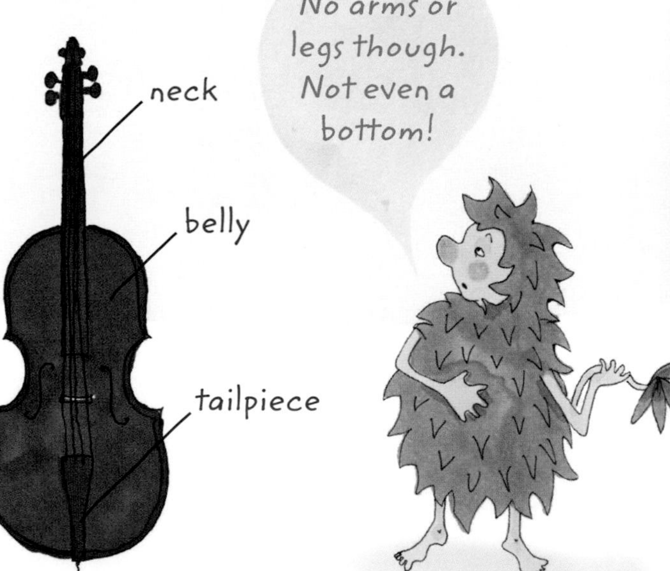

The shape of the instruments is a bit like the shape of a female human body. Parts of them have the same names: neck, back and belly.

'Pitch' means how **high** or **low** the instruments sound. Each instrument in the String Family has its own, clear range of pitch.

So all the string instruments are like one big tree, and together they make a big sound!

The range of pitch in the string family is very wide: the instruments go from a very high sound to a very low sound.

The Pitch Tree: High Sounds to Low Sounds

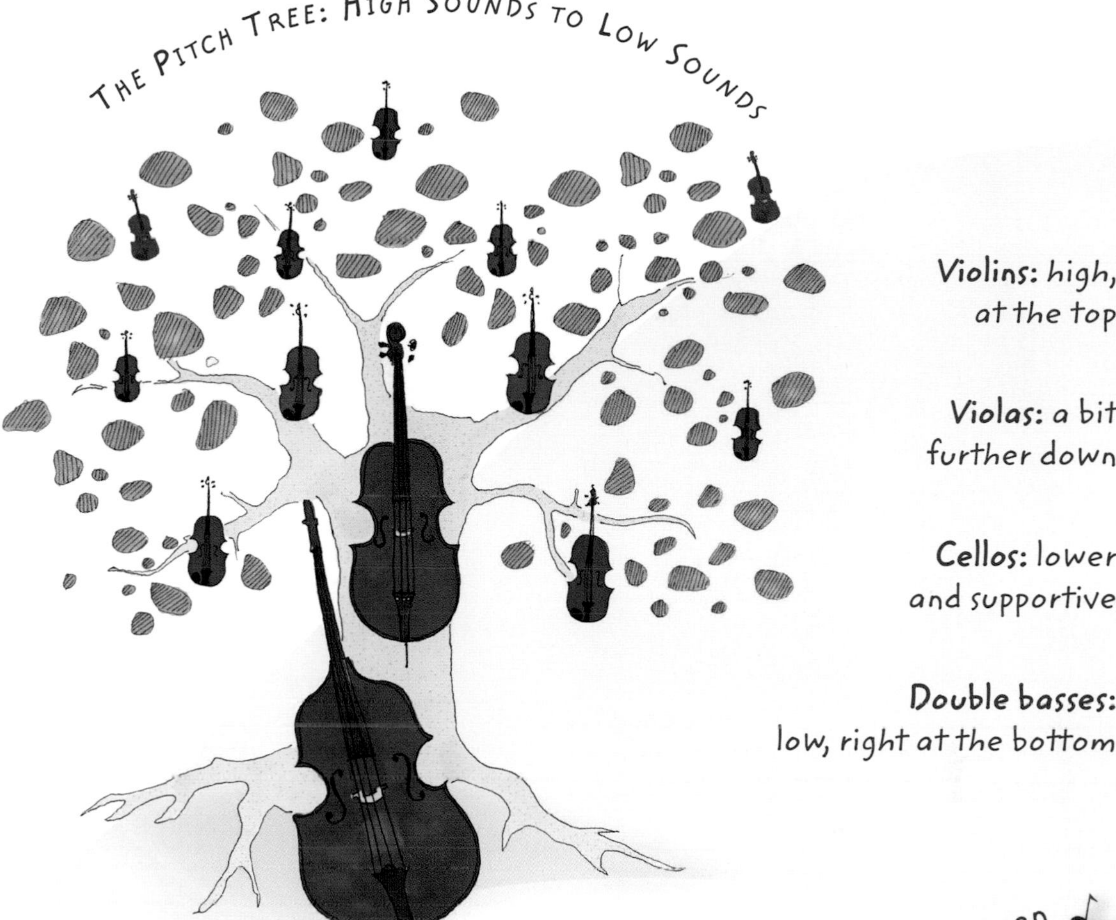

Violins: high, at the top

Violas: a bit further down

Cellos: lower and supportive

Double basses: low, right at the bottom

Listen 4

STRING FAMILY TOGETHER – BOWED

Felix **Mendelssohn**
String Symphony No. 2
I. Allegro (extract)
String instruments together playing cheerful music!

You can pluck the strings too – I like doing that! It's like pinging a piece of elastic.

Listen 5

STRING FAMILY TOGETHER – PIZZICATO

Johann **Strauss II**
Pizzicato Polka (extract)

Instead of using their bows, the players are all plucking the strings: it is 'pizzicato'. Bouncy!

Violin

People say that the violin 'sings'. If somebody sings to you, it can make you feel happy or sad. The sound of the violin is like that too.

Sometimes it can make you forget everything around you, as if it's casting a wonderful spell on you!

In an orchestra, the violinist at the front is the 'leader' (or 'concert master') of the whole group.

In a big orchestra, there could be 16 *first* violins, playing the highest-sounding part, and 14 *second* violins, playing a part that sounds a bit lower.

VIOLIN SOLO

This music is part of a story about Carmen, a beautiful Spanish gypsy. Listen to the violin twirling around, up high and down low: Carmen is showing off!

Pablo de **Sarasate**
Carmen Fantasy

CARMEN THE GYPSY

PABLO DE SARASATE

Sarasate was a Spanish composer and Carmen was a beautiful Spanish gypsy.

VIOLINS TOGETHER

The violins are busy here. All the bows rush backwards and forwards, playing a happy dance for a shepherd girl.

Hugo **Alfvén**
The Mountain King
Dance of the Shepherd Girl (extract)

Viola

Violas look exactly like violins but they're slightly bigger. You play them the same way.

Because the viola is BIGGER than the violin, it sounds LOWER.

FRANZ ANTON HOFFMEISTER
Hoffmeister lived in Vienna and was friends with Mozart.

VIOLA SOLO

The viola has a chance to shine in this cheerful music.

Franz Anton **Hoffmeister**
Viola Concerto
III. Rondo: Allegro

So while the violins sing out the tune at the top, the violas strengthen it underneath with a lovely deep, rich sound.

There are about 12 violas in a big orchestra.

VIOLAS TOGETHER

All the violas together, playing a mysterious melody: the sound is in between the high violins and the low cellos.

Gustav **Mahler**
Symphony No. 10
I. Adagio (extract)

Cello

Cellos are like *very* big violins. The players – cellists – sit down to play them.

Cellists still hold the bow in their right hand and the instrument in their left hand, but the cello is balanced on the floor.

I like pinging – oops, I mean PLUCKING – the strings! It's even more fun than popping bubble-wrap!

It has a spike poking out of the bottom which helps to stop it slipping.

Okay, so you can't put a cello under your chin like a violin. Ouch!

THE COMPOSER

Listen 10

CELLO SOLO

The cello is singing!

Alexander **Glazunov**
Serenade espagnole

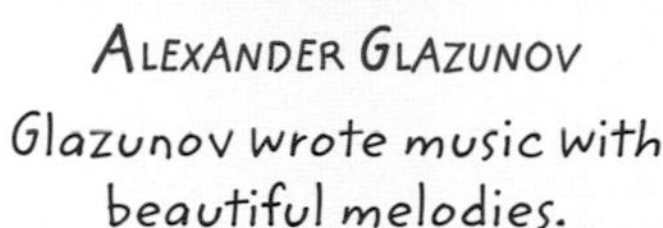

ALEXANDER GLAZUNOV

Glazunov wrote music with beautiful melodies.

The violin sings up high, but the cello sings just as beautifully lower down.

It's like chocolate in sound! Rich and irresistible.

There are about 10 cellos in a big orchestra.

Oh I love the cello... but I want to go home! Where's my favourite music? Let's keep going and find it!

CELLOS TOGETHER

All the cellos build from the bottom to the top, where they get an answer from the flutes. Then they do it again – as if they are peeling back a curtain... what can you see?

Giuseppe **Verdi**
Requiem
Offertorio (extract)

Double Bass

Double basses are enormous. They are about 180 cm (six feet) from bottom to top – like a very tall person. And they are wide, too!

The word 'double', here, is like the word 'extra': it means that they sound really low.

They have a very low sound, so their pitch is right at the bottom. They are the roots of the orchestra!

Plucking *these* strings is great! They make a big bonging sound.

Double basses look like their relatives – the violins, violas and cellos – but their shape is a bit different. For example, their shoulders slope a bit more.

There are about eight double basses in a big orchestra.

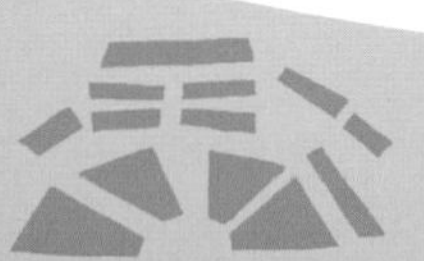

Listen 12

Double Bass Solo

The double bass can play a melody too, but it doesn't get many melodies to play in the orchestra.

Giovanni **Bottesini**

Double Bass Concertino in C minor

III. Finale: Allegro (extract)

THE COMPOSER

Giovanni Bottesini

Bottesini was a brilliant double bass player. His music shows what this huge instrument can do on its own.

I think it's too big for me...

Listen 13

Double Basses Together

It's not often that you hear the whole double bass section on its own. Here it is – deep, deep down!

Richard **Strauss**

Also sprach Zarathustra

VI. Song of Science (extract)

Flutes Oboes Clarinets Bassoons

Woodwind

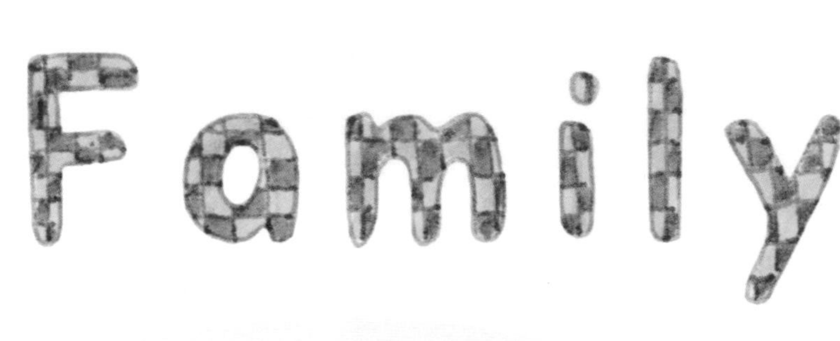

There are strong characters in this family. Unlike the String Family, each instrument in the Woodwind Family sounds very different.

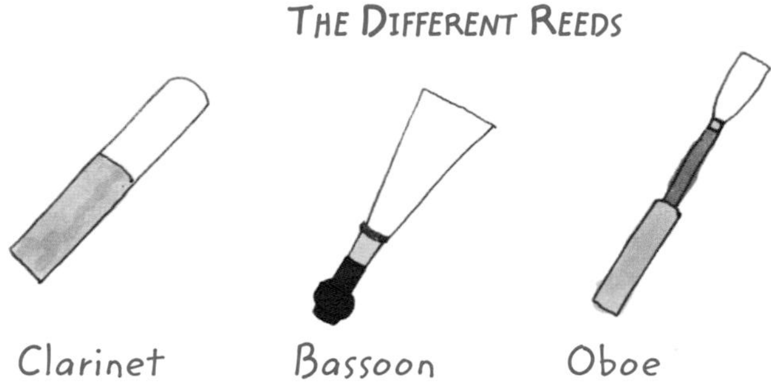

Well, to start with, they are all long tubes that you blow down to make a sound.

Most of them are made of wood, but the modern flute is made of metal. They have a mouthpiece as well as keys for different notes.

In the orchestra, woodwind instruments often come in pairs: two flutes, two oboes, two clarinets, two bassoons.

Then there are extra ones, like the piccolo – a tiny flute.

The Colour Palette

If we imagine the sound of each woodwind instrument to be like a colour, this is what the woodwind colour palette might look like:

Listen 14

Woodwind Together

Here is the woodwind family playing together, along with the French horn. The French horn is a brass instrument but it sounds good with woodwind instruments: it helps to makes a nice round sound.

Carl **Reinecke**
Wind Octet
IV. Finale
(extract)

In music for the orchestra there are a lot of solos for the woodwind: that's when these special sounds have a chance to shine.

Flute

You can even get really expensive flutes made of gold!

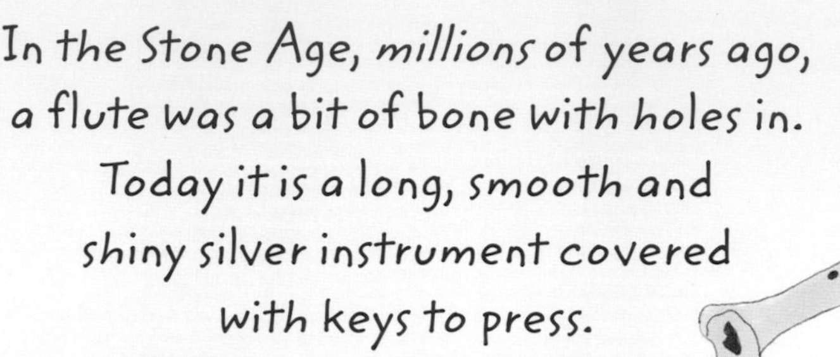

In the Stone Age, *millions* of years ago, a flute was a bit of bone with holes in. Today it is a long, smooth and shiny silver instrument covered with keys to press.

To play the flute, you hold it sideways and blow across the hole – the mouthpiece. It's like blowing across the top of a bottle.

Piccolo

In a full orchestra, there are two flutes and often a piccolo too: a little flute that sounds very high.

The flute can play music that flutters around all over the place like a butterfly.

Flute Solo

A concerto (a piece for a solo instrument and orchestra) by one of J.S. Bach's many sons. After the introduction, listen to the fast notes of the flute above the orchestra.

Carl Philipp Emanuel **Bach**
Flute Concerto in A major, Wq. 168
III. *Allegro assai*

I'm having so much fun, it doesn't matter that I haven't found my favourite music yet! There are so many lovely things to listen to!

THE COMPOSER

Carl Philipp Emanuel Bach

C.P.E. Bach, son of the great Johann Sebastian Bach, didn't simply copy his father: his own music was fresh and new.

Listen

Flutes Together

The composer Smetana is describing in music a great river: can you imagine the rippling water? The flutes are playing together.

Bedřich **Smetana**
Ma vlást
II. Vltava (The Moldau)
(extract)

Oboe

The oboe's bright, clear sound can fly through the orchestra like an arrow.

The oboe gets a solo before the concert has even started! It plays the note 'A' for the rest of the orchestra.

All the other instruments have to make sure that their 'A' is exactly the same as the oboe's 'A'.

This is called 'tuning up'.

You put your lips around a reed to blow down the oboe. This reed is a double-reed: two very thin slices of cane (a kind of woody grass) that vibrate against each other when you blow.

Have you ever tried to blow through a blade of grass? It's the same idea. The grass vibrates and it makes a loud squeak.

Oboe Solo

The masterful Mozart having fun with the oboe. Sometimes the oboe plays a tune and then the orchestra answers it. Can you hear that happen at the beginning of the piece? All the way through, it's as if the oboe is telling a story to the orchestra, and the orchestra is listening and nodding and reacting.

Wolfgang Amadeus **Mozart**
Oboe Concerto
III. Allegro

Wolfgang Amadeus Mozart

Mozart didn't play the oboe but he still composed one of the most important pieces ever written for the instrument.

In a famous piece called *Peter and the Wolf*, by Prokofiev, the oboe takes the part of the duck!

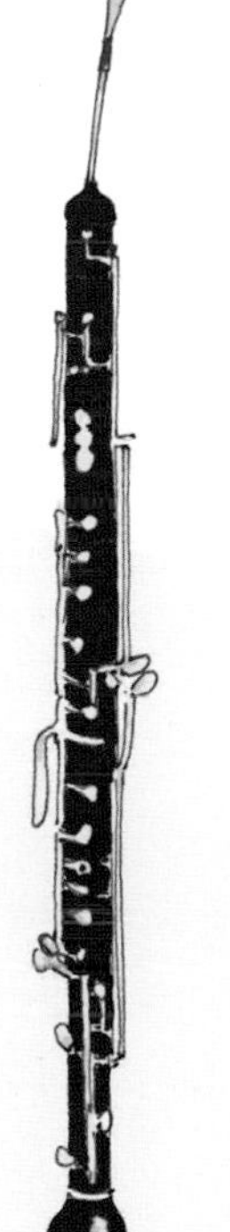

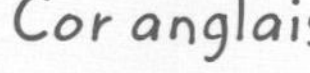
Cor anglais

There are usually two oboes in a full orchestra, and often a cor anglais.

The cor anglais is like a bigger oboe, and it makes a sort of sad, lonely sound.

Listen
18

Oboes Together

Two oboes with music from a ballet. It is about a shepherdess and a goatherd who love each other, and it has a happy ending!

Maurice **Ravel**
Daphnis et Chloé
Part III: Pantomime (extract)

Clarinet

Clarinets are cool! Sometimes they play jazz music, and they seem kind of knowing and strong.

The clarinet makes a really smooth sound.

The clarinet has a single reed. This is attached to a solid mouthpiece. You put your lips around the mouthpiece and reed to blow down the instrument.

Beginners sometimes make a squeak by mistake!

Squeak!

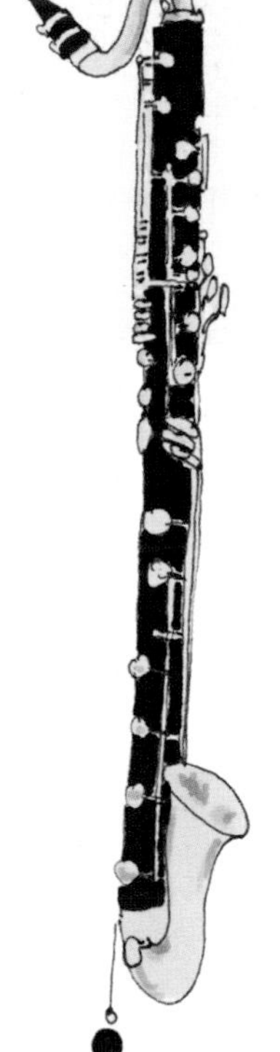

There are often two clarinets in a big orchestra and sometimes a bass clarinet too — a really big one that sounds very low.

The silver bits look complicated! But only some of them are keys you need to press.

Bass clarinet

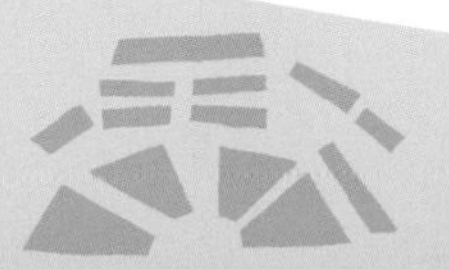

THE COMPOSER

AARON COPLAND

Copland came from the USA, where jazz music was born. Can you hear how much he liked jazz?

CLARINET SOLO

Here is the confident, cheeky clarinet playing with string instruments. The music is spiky and fun... keep listening – you never quite know what's going to happen next!

Aaron **Copland**
Clarinet Concerto
Rather Fast (extract)

Listen 20

CLARINETS TOGETHER

Two clarinets together playing gentler music by Mendelssohn.

Felix **Mendelssohn**
The Hebrides ('Fingal's Cave')
(extract)

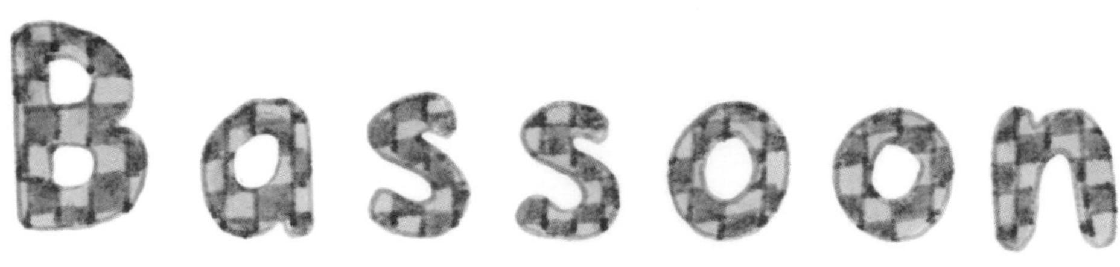

In Italian the bassoon is called a 'fagotto'! If you were an Italian, you would be saying 'Oh, I'm sorry, I forgot my fagotto today!'

'Bassoon' – what a funny name!

But this instrument is like a lovely soft carpet in the orchestra. In this book we've given it the colour of dark red: it is warm and welcoming.

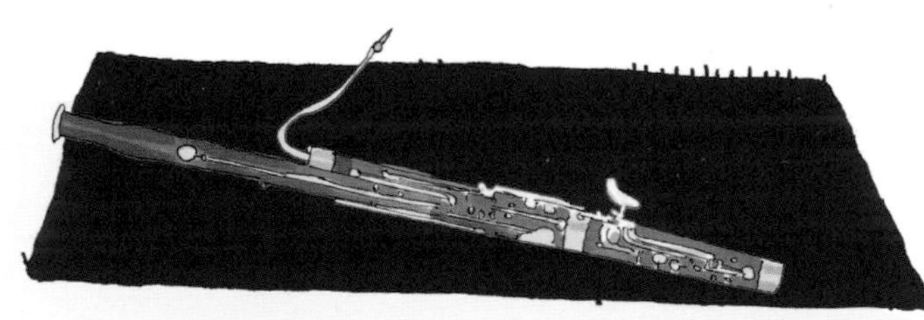

Most of the time it sounds low down, but sometimes it has a solo and sings out higher.

There are two bassoons and often a contrabassoon in a big orchestra: the contrabassoon is even bigger and sounds even lower.

Contrabassoon

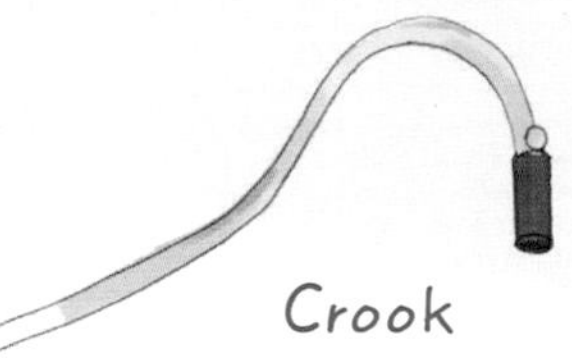

Crook

The bassoon has a double reed, like the oboe, but it is on the end of a 'crook'.

THE COMPOSER

ANTONIO VIVALDI

This is just one of Vivaldi's 500 concertos. He was a busy man!

BASSOON SOLO

Many years ago, Vivaldi knew something very important: the bassoon could be a lovely solo instrument. Because it has a low pitch, people sometimes forget how nicely it can sing! Don't you think it makes a friendly sound?

Antonio **Vivaldi**
Bassoon Concerto in F major, RV 486
I. Allegro

The bassoon does have solos but it isn't dying to show off all the time. People who play the bassoon (bassoonists) are often the same – relaxed and friendly.

Four sections are joined together to make the bassoon: the bell, the tenor joint, the bass joint and the... um... butt joint!

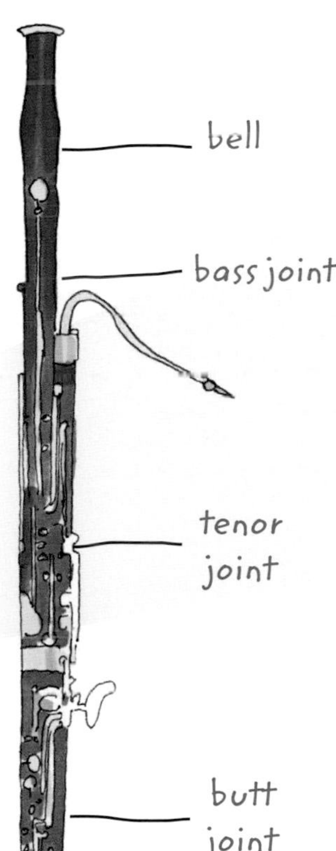

BASSOONS TOGETHER

Two bassoons have a little duet in the Concerto for Orchestra by the Hungarian composer Bartók.

Béla **Bartók**
Concerto for Orchestra
II. Game of the Pairs (extract)

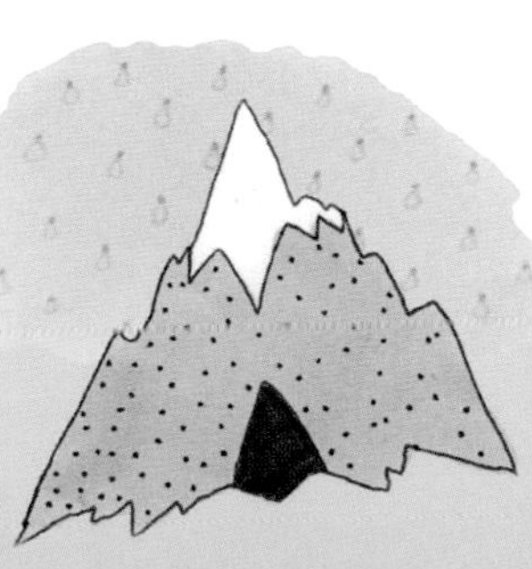

Brass Family

Trumpets French Horns Trombones Tuba

This big, beefy, golden section near the back has no problem being heard!

The instruments sound strong and bold.

These are all shiny instruments made of brass metal. It looks like gold!

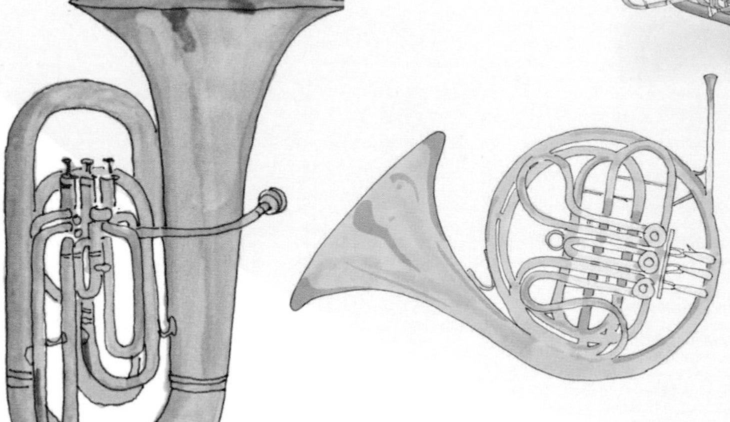

Tuba

French horn

Trombone

Trumpet

The air that you blow into them whizzes round all those bends and twists, and bursts out of the bell-shaped end as a sound.

They all have brass tubes coiled round like snakes.

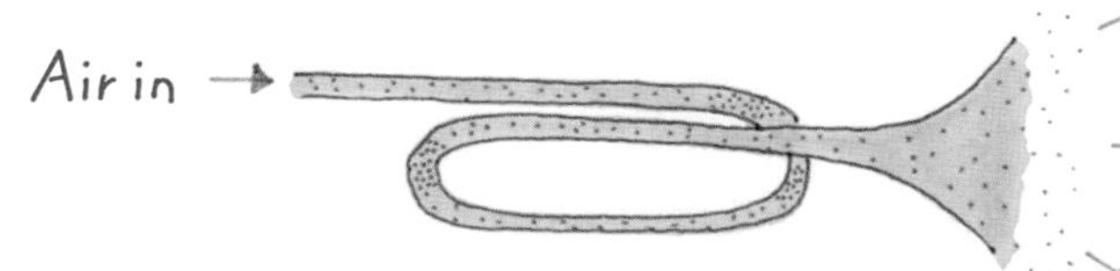

For producing different notes, the trombone has a 'slide' and the trumpet, French horn and tuba have valves to press.

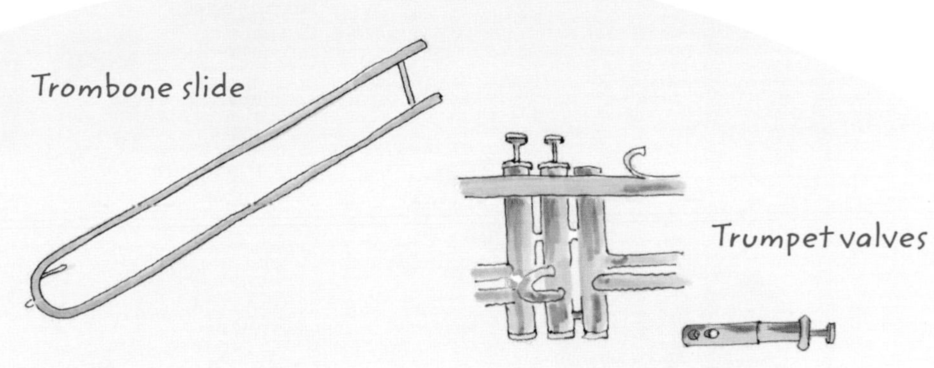

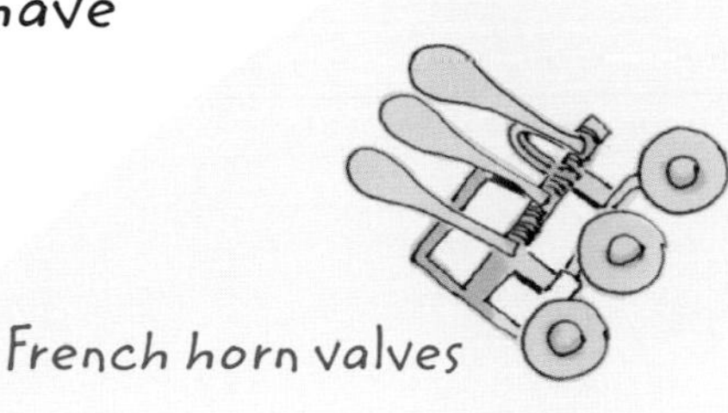

The player's body controls the sound too: the lips and the diaphragm – a muscle underneath your lungs.

You blow down brass instruments as you do down woodwind instruments, but the mouthpieces are different. You don't put your mouth *round* a brass mouthpiece: you put your lips together and against it, then blow.

Tormod likes blowing this way against his hand instead of a mouthpiece: it makes a funny noise. Can you do it too?

Listen 23

Brass Family Together

All the brass instruments together can make this wonderful, powerful sound.

Hector **Berlioz**
Requiem
II. Dies irae (extract)

Trumpet

Trumpets are bold and bossy.
Their sound is clear and bright.

There are often three trumpets in the orchestra. When they play together, with their brass bells in the air, it's an exciting sound!

The trumpet has three 'piston' valves. You press these down to make different notes sound, but you have to use your lips and diaphragm as well.

Shiny, bossy... and loud! I love trumpets!

Listen 24

TRUMPET SOLO

The bold trumpet is the solo instrument, and sounds a bit cheeky here!

Johann Nepomuk **Hummel**
Trumpet Concerto
III. Rondo

THE COMPOSER

JOHANN NEPOMUK HUMMEL

Hummel came from Vienna and was friends with the great Beethoven.

Oh, I dream of home... I can hear my favourite music in my head but I can't find it here...

Listen 25

TRUMPETS TOGETHER

You can hear the strong trumpets clearly in this exciting music by the film composer John Williams.

John **Williams**
Raiders of the Lost Ark
Main Title Theme (extract)

French Horn

The French horn is coiled round in a kind of circle. The sound can be smooth and velvety but also loud and energetic!

Hundreds of years ago, horns were used by people who went out hunting on horseback. The horns could be heard a long way away.

In the orchestra today, they get big, rousing solos.

There could be four or five horns in the orchestra.

While they blow down the mouthpiece, players also put one hand into the bell of the horn – the big, wide part at the end – to control the sound.

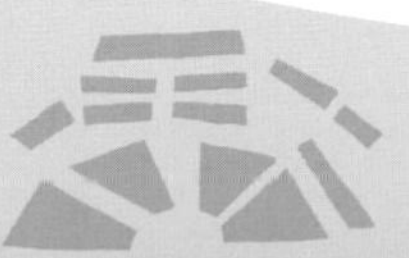

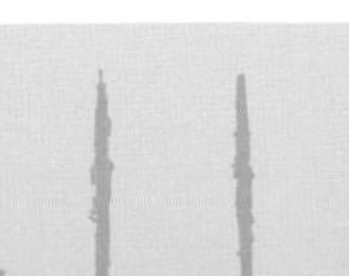

THE COMPOSER

WOLFGANG AMADEUS MOZART

Mozart was full of energy and enthusiasm, and his music is often the same!

Listen 26

FRENCH HORN SOLO

Mozart is making the French horn sound playful in his Horn Concerto No. 4.

Wolfgang Amadeus **Mozart**
Horn Concerto No. 4
III. Rondo: Allegro vivace

The horn has three 'rotary' valves – they're different from the trumpet and tuba's 'piston' valves. I think they ping up and down more easily!

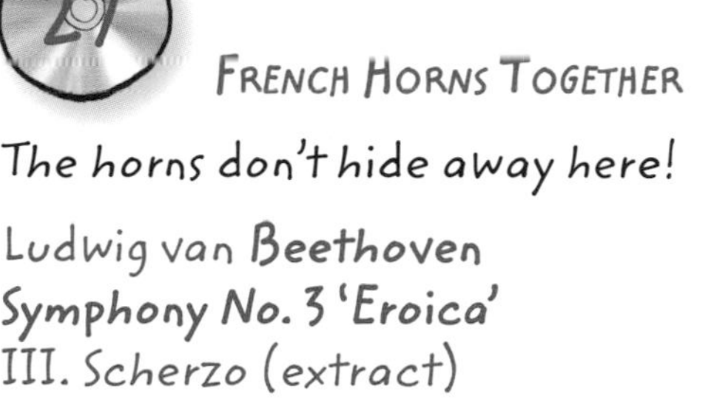

Listen 27

FRENCH HORNS TOGETHER

The horns don't hide away here!

Ludwig van **Beethoven**
Symphony No. 3 'Eroica'
III. Scherzo (extract)

Trombone

The trombone is known for its slide: a long piece of tube that you pull out and push in, to play different notes.

How does the slide actually work? Well, when you push it out, you make the tube **longer** and that makes the sound **lower.**

When you pull it in, you make the tube **shorter** and that makes the sound **higher.**

There could be three trombones in the orchestra. For some music, you might see more than three.

There are other sizes of trombone besides the normal 'tenor' one, including a big and booming bass trombone.

Listen 28

TROMBONE SOLO

The trombone can sound cool too. It's jazzy here...

Ástor **Piazzolla**, arr. G. Senanes
Serie del angel
I. La muerte del angel

ÁSTOR PIAZZOLLA

Piazzolla came from Argentina where the tango has been danced for years. He loved the tango!

TROMBONES TOGETHER

Wagner was an expert at getting the most out of the trombones!

Richard **Wagner**
Tannhäuser
Overture (extract)

Trombones often play together in a group. You can see their shiny tubes being lifted up at the back of the orchestra as the players get ready. Then... in and out go the slides at the same time – and what a fantastic sound!

Tuba

Tubas are so big, the players have to hug them when they play!

The sound of the tuba is gentle and strong. It can simply go 'oom-pah, oom-pah' underneath everything else, but it can play complicated things too.

Even though it's big and heavy, the tuba can play really fast notes. But you need a lot of puff to make it happen!

The orchestra only needs one tuba! The sound is very low down and you don't hear it on its own very much in orchestral music.

TUBA SOLO

The big tuba sounds powerful but warm and friendly too. It doesn't often get to be the soloist: it's making the most of it here.

Ralph **Vaughan Williams**
Tuba Concerto
I. Prelude

THE COMPOSER

RALPH VAUGHAN WILLIAMS

Vaughan Williams was English and he loved England's folk music. He used some of it in his own compositions.

What a big bear of an instrument! But I still don't hear my favourite music. When will we find it?

Percussion

There are many percussion instruments. They can be shaken, tapped, stroked, knocked... and they make all kinds of different sounds.

Xylophone

So these are the main percussion instruments. Only a few of these appear in the orchestra at the same time.

Timpani (or 'Kettledrums')

This family is good at RHYTHM. If you hear and feel the beat of music, you often want to tap your foot or click your fingers. Playing percussion is like doing that with instruments!

I'm playing my special piece of music on the triangle! I'm sure we're going to find it soon.

Snare drum (or 'Side drum')

Triangle

Some music for orchestra has a lot of percussion. It's like splashing colour on a painting!

Bass drum

Tuned – Produce Different Notes

Xylophone

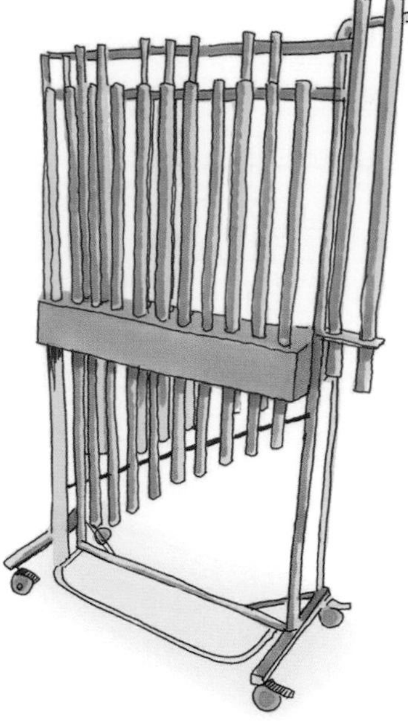

Tubular bells (or 'Chimes')

Celesta (or 'Celeste')

Timpani
(or 'Kettledrums')

Glockenspiel

Vibraphone

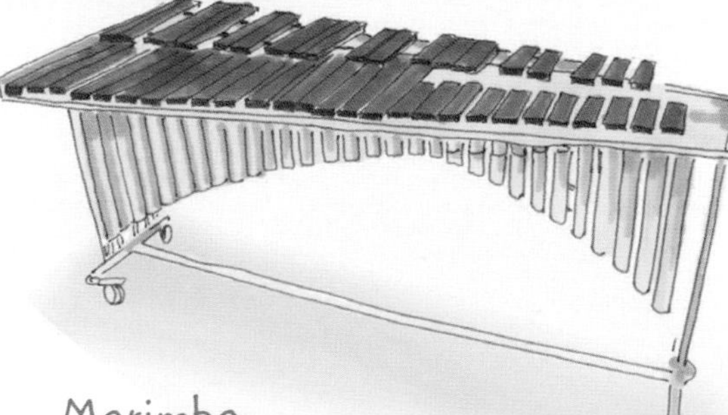

Marimba

Listen 31

Tuned Percussion Instruments

Listen to a quick example of each tuned percussion instrument.

Untuned – Produce One Sound Only

Actually the percussion section *could* include anything – even Tormod's head if it's loud enough when you hit it – but it's very unusual to have instruments that are not the 'normal' ones.

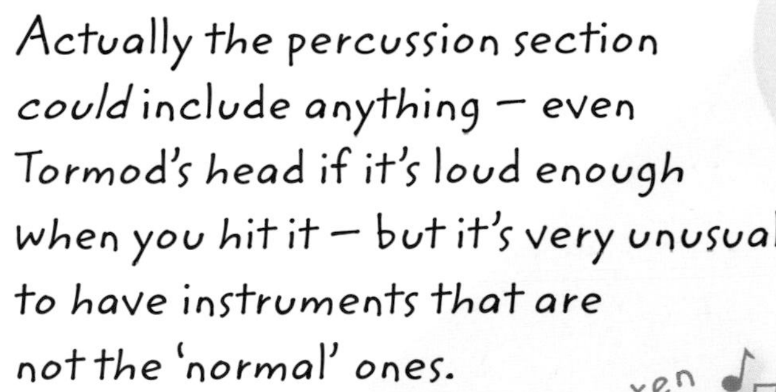

So if I hit my head, is my head percussion? Owwww!

Tambourine

Triangle

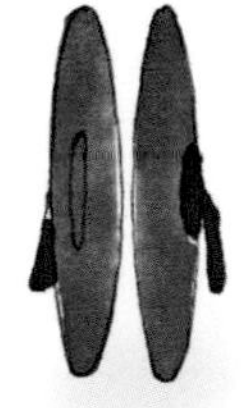

Cymbals

Listen 32

Untuned Percussion Instruments

Listen to a quick example of each untuned percussion instrument.

Wood block

Maracas

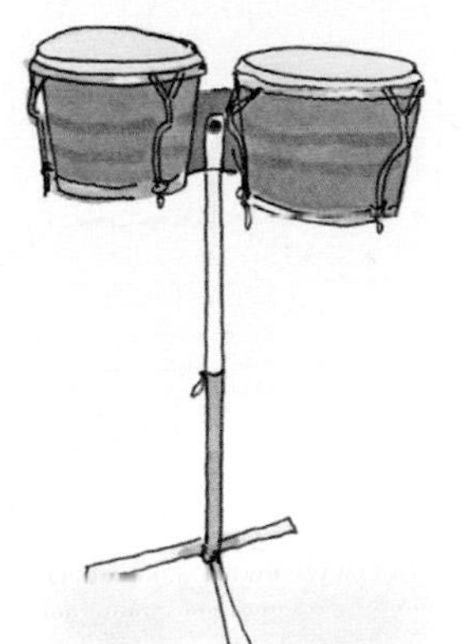

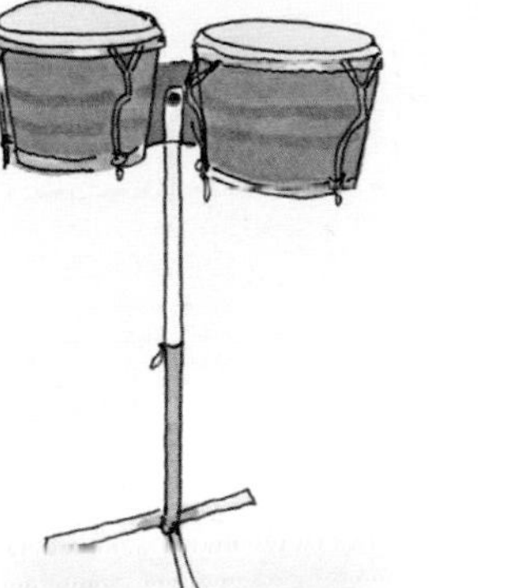

Bongos

Castanets

Listen 33

Percussion Together

Here are just a few of the percussion instruments playing together in a fierce and fiery dance.

Aram Il'yich **Khachaturian**

Gayane

Sabre Dance (extract)

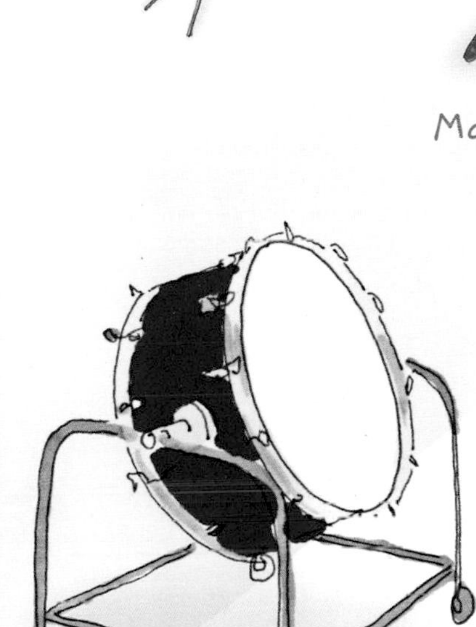

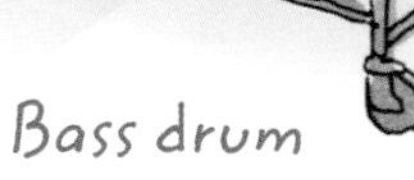

Bass drum

Snare drum (or 'Side drum')

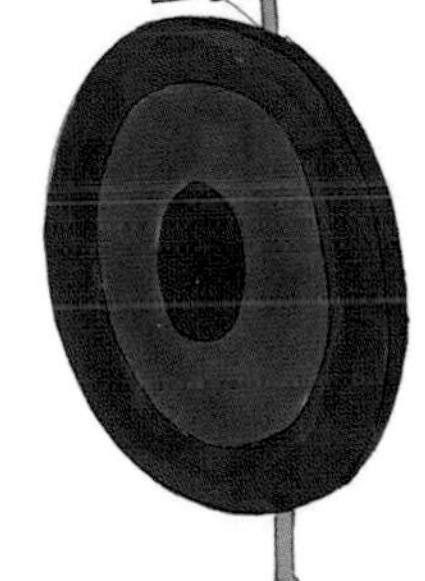

Tam-tam

Tom-toms

SAXOPHONE SOLO

The saxophone has the solo here, with the orchestra. Can you also hear a snare drum at the beginning, then a wood block at 0:33? It's a lively piece.

Darius **Milhaud**
Scaramouche
III. Brazileira

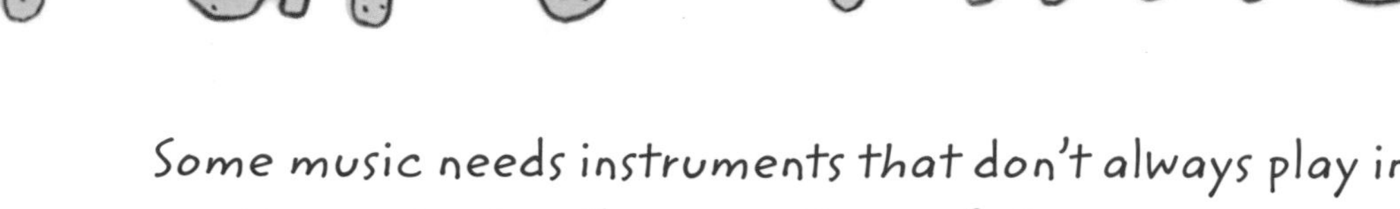

Some music needs instruments that don't always play in the orchestra. Here are three of these instruments.

The saxophone is part of the woodwind section. It's made of brass, but it has a reed – like the clarinet's reed.

Members

Saxophone Harp Piano

The harp is a string instrument, but it isn't like the violin or cello. It's a different shape, it's much bigger, and you always pluck the strings.

The piano is almost like an orchestra on its own! When it plays in the orchestra, it adds another kind of sound.

Listen 36

PIANO SOLO

I bet you recognise this tune! Yes, it's *Twinkle, Twinkle, Little Star*. But wait... the composer then gives the tune 'variations,' which is a bit like dressing it up in different clothes. So it starts to sound faster and more complicated. Listen to the piano take off with it!

Ernő **Dohnányi**
Variations on a Nursery Song
Theme & Variation 1

How about a duet? You and me?

HARP SOLO

The harp sounds completely free in this gentle piece. Imagine you are running across fields as you listen, with the wind in your hair!

Claude **Debussy**
Deux Danses
No. 2 Danse profane

The Conductor

This is the boss! Back to the audience, front to the orchestra, the conductor is in charge.

The conductor's job is to make the orchestra a really good team. With a lot of players, the music could sound messy. So the conductor keeps everyone together.

The most obvious job for a conductor in guiding the orchestra is to 'beat time'. That stops the players from going too slowly or too fast.

Some conductors hold a stick – a baton – and some don't.

Some conductors bounce up and down and make weird faces! They have to do whatever they can so that the music doesn't sound like a big splodge.

EDVARD GRIEG

The Norwegian composer Edvard Grieg said he didn't like listening to 'In the Hall of the Mountain King,' even though he created it himself. But many other people love it!

TORMOD'S FAVOURITE MUSIC

Grieg wrote this music for a play by fellow Norwegian Henrik Ibsen called *Peer Gynt*. The play is based on a fairytale. Peer Gynt is in the mountains and enters the royal hall of the Old Man (the Mountain King): it is full of trolls, gnomes and goblins!

Edvard **Grieg**
Peer Gynt
In the Hall of the Mountain King

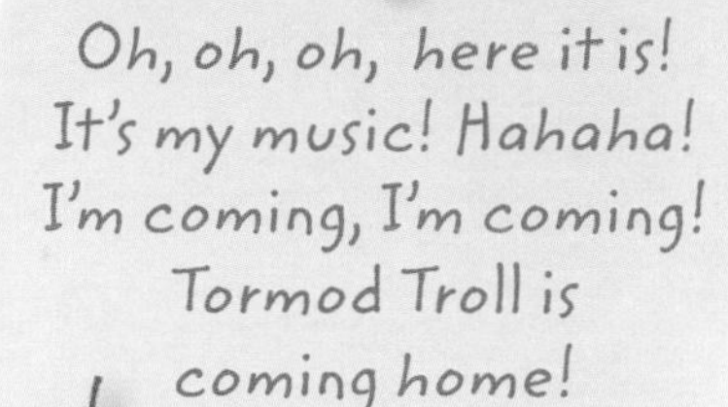

Oh, oh, oh, here it is!
It's my music! Hahaha!
I'm coming, I'm coming!
Tormod Troll is
coming home!

Ah, it's been a long, long life for me on this mountain.
Didn't you bring a harp?
I need a triangle!
Oh yeah! I want an instrumen too!
I want to go, I want to go!
Where have I been? I've been exploring the ORCHESTRA! The most amazing team in music!

I'm going
to find a
golden trumpet
to match
my fur!
Ooh, is that
a bassoon?
1-2, 1-2,
don't stop,
dop-dop,
1-2, 1-2...

1. What is the orchestra grouped into?
a. Families
b. Packs
c. Houses

2. Which family in the orchestra has members that look and sound similar?
a. The String Family
b. The Percussion Family
c. The Woodwind Family

3. What do you press on trumpets, horns and tubas?
a. Buttons
b. Keys
c. Valves

4. What do you press on woodwind instruments?
a. Buttons
b. Keys
c. Valves

5. Which part of an animal has the same name as a brass instrument?
a. Hoof
b. Wing
c. Horn

6. Why are wind instruments called wind instruments?
a. Because they make a rude noise
b. Because you blow air down them
c. Because they are always loud

7. Which best describes the pitch of the double bass?
a. High up
b. In the middle
c. Low down

8. What is a tuba made of?
a. Gold
b. Wood
c. Brass

9. Why is the oboe always the first instrument you hear in a concert?
a. Because oboists are show-offs
b. Because the oboe's 'A' is used for tuning up
c. Because the oboe is more important than other instruments

10. Which mathematical shape has the same name as an instrument?
a. Triangle
b. Circle
c. Square

11. Which is the smallest instrument in the string family?
a. Cello
b. Violin
c. Viola

12. What does the conductor hold when conducting?
a. A baguette
b. A baton
c. A banger

13. What is the bit at the end of a string player's bow called?
a. Frog
b. Toad
c. Fish

14. What instrument does the leader or concertmaster play?
a. Violin
b. Flute
c. Trumpet

15. What is the point of the conductor?
a. There isn't one
b. To shout loudly
c. To keep everyone together

16. What is the other name for the timpani?
a. Kettledrums
b. Coffeedrums
c. Pepperdrums

17. What is a reed made of?
a. Paper
b. Cane
c. Plastic

18. What does 'pizzicato' mean?
a. Watching the conductor
b. Listening carefully
c. Plucking the strings

19. What does a trombone have?
a. A see-saw
b. A swing
c. A slide

20. What is the very small flute called?
a. Pomelo
b. Piccolo
c. Pedalo

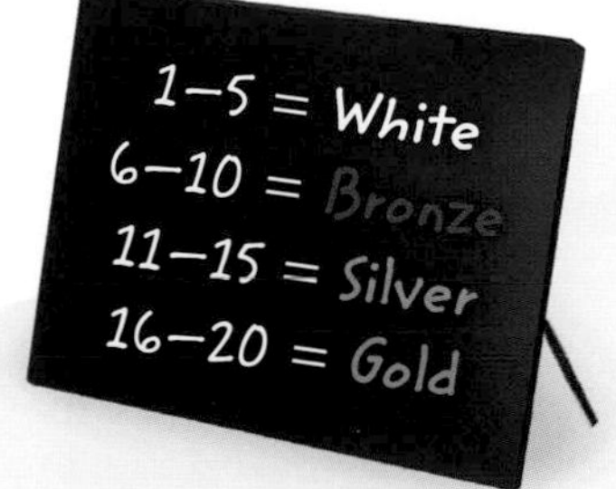

Answers 1. a, 2. a, 3. c, 4. b, 5. c, 6. b, 7. c, 8. c, 9. b, 10. a, 11. b, 12. b, 13. a, 14. a, 15. c, 16. a, 17. b, 18. c, 19. c, 20. b

Track List

1 Tormod's Favourite Music
Edvard **Grieg** (1843–1907)
'In the Hall of the Mountain King' from *Peer Gynt* Suite No. 1 — 2:23
Norrköping Symphony Orchestra; Mats Rondin — 8.578203

2 Full Orchestra
Wolfgang Amadeus **Mozart** (1756–1791)
Overture to *The Magic Flute* (extract) — 1:50
Budapest Failoni Chamber Orchestra; Michael Halász — 8.660030–31

3 Full Orchestra
Pyotr Il'yich **Tchaikovsky** (1840–1893)
'Russian Dance' from *The Nutcracker* — 1:06
Slovak Philharmonic Orchestra; Ondrej Lenárd — 8.553271

4 String Family – Bowed
Felix **Mendelssohn** (1809–1847)
String Symphony No. 2 in D major (I. Allegro) (extract) — 1:00
Northern Chamber Orchestra; Nicholas Ward — 8.553161

5 String Family – Pizzicato
Johann **Strauss II** (1825–1899)
Pizzicato Polka (extract) — 0:30
Slovak Radio Symphony Orchestra; Ondrej Lenárd — 8.550337

6 Violin Solo
Pablo de **Sarasate** (1844–1908)
Carmen Fantasy, Op. 25 — 2:59
Tianwa Yang, violin; Orquesta Sinfónica de Navarra;
Ernest Martínez Izquierdo — 8.572216

7 Violins Together
Hugo **Alfvén** (1872–1960)
'Dance of the Shepherd Girl' from *The Mountain King* (extract) — 0:38
Royal Scottish National Orchestra; Niklas Willén — 8.553962

8 Viola Solo
Franz Anton **Hoffmeister** (1754–1812)
Viola Concerto in B flat major (III. Rondo: Allegro) — 4:01
Victoria Chiang, viola; Baltimore Chamber Orchestra;
Markand Thakar — 8.572162

9 Violas Together
Gustav **Mahler** (1860–1911)
Symphony No. 10 (I. Adagio) (extract) — 0:39
Polish National Radio Symphony Orchestra; Robert Olson — 8.554811

10 Cello Solo
Alexander **Glazunov** (1865–1936)
Serenade espagnole, Op. 20 No. 2 — 2:59
Alexander Rudin, cello; Moscow Symphony Orchestra;
Igor Golovchin — 8.555764

11 Cellos Together
Giuseppe **Verdi** (1813–1891)
Requiem (Offertorio) (extract) — 0:43
Hungarian State Opera Orchestra; Pier Giorgio Morandi — 8.550944–45

12 Double Bass Solo
Giovanni **Bottesini** (1821–1889)
Double Bass Concertino in C minor (III. Finale: Allegro) (extract) — 2:24
Thomas Martin, double bass; London Symphony Orchestra;
Franco Petracchi — 8.570398

13 Double Basses Together
Richard **Strauss** (1864–1949)
Also sprach Zarathustra (VI. 'Song of Science') (extract) — 0:43
Slovak Philharmonic Orchestra; Zdeněk Košler — 8.550182

14 Woodwind Family
Carl **Reinecke** (1824–1910)
Wind Octet, Op. 21 (IV. Finale: Allegro molto e grazioso) (extract) — 0:49
Members of the Boston Symphony Orchestra — 8.570777

15 Flute Solo
Carl Philipp Emanuel **Bach** (1714–1788)
Flute Concerto in A major, Wq. 168, H. 438 (III. Allegro assai) — 5:09
Patrick Gallois, flute; Toronto Chamber Orchestra; Kevin Mallon — 8.555715–16

16 Flutes Together
Bedřich **Smetana** (1824–1884)
Ma vlást (II. 'Vltava' – 'The Moldau') (extract) — 0:38
Polish National Radio Symphony Orchestra; Antoni Wit — 8.550931

17 Oboe Solo
Wolfgang Amadeus **Mozart** (1756–1791)
Oboe Concerto in C major, K. 314 (III. Allegro) — 3:46
Martin Gabriel, oboe; Vienna Mozart Academy; Johannes Wildner — 8.550345

18 Oboes Together
Maurice **Ravel** (1875–1937)
Daphnis et Chloé (Part III: 'Pantomime') (extract) — 0:16
Orchestre National de Lyon; Jun Märkl — 8.570992

19 **Clarinet Solo**
Aaron **Copland** (1900–1990)
Clarinet Concerto (Rather Fast) (extract) 5:36
Laura Ardan, clarinet; Nashville Chamber Orchestra; Paul Gambill 8.559069

20 **Clarinets Together**
Felix **Mendelssohn** (1809–1847)
The Hebrides ('Fingal's Cave'), Op. 26 (extract) 0:44
Slovak Philharmonic Orchestra; Oliver Dohnányi 8.554433

21 **Bassoon Solo**
Antonio **Vivaldi** (1678–1741)
Bassoon Concerto in F major, RV 486 (I. Allegro) 3:14
Tamás Benkócs, bassoon; Nicolaus Esterházy Sinfonia; Béla Drahos 8.555938

22 **Bassoons Together**
Béla **Bartók** (1881–1945)
Concerto for Orchestra (II. 'Game of the Pairs') (extract) 0:24
Belgian Radio and Television Philharmonic Orchestra; Alexander Rahbari 8.550261

23 **Brass Family**
Hector **Berlioz** (1803–1869)
Requiem, Op. 5 (II. Dies irae) (extract) 1:06
Elora Festival Orchestra; Noel Edison 8.554494–95

24 **Trumpet Solo**
Johann Nepomuk **Hummel** (1778–1837)
Trumpet Concerto in E major, S49 (III. Rondo) 3:43
Niklas Eklund, trumpet; Swedish Chamber Orchestra; Roy Goodman 8.554806

25 **Trumpets Together**
John **Williams** (b. 1932)
Raiders of the Lost Ark (Main Title Theme) (extract) 0:36
Royal Liverpool Philharmonic Orchestra; Carl Davis 8.570505

26 **French Horn Solo**
Wolfgang Amadeus **Mozart** (1756–1791)
Horn Concerto No. 4 in E flat, K. 495 (III. Rondo: Allegro vivace) 3:37
Jacek Muzyk, horn; Amadeus Chamber Orchestra of Polish Radio;
Agnieszka Duczmal 8.570419

27 **French Horns Together**
Ludwig van **Beethoven** (1770–1827)
Symphony No. 3 'Eroica' (III. Scherzo: Allegro vivace) (extract) 0:23
Nicolaus Esterházy Sinfonia; Béla Drahos 8.553475

28 **Trombone Solo**
Ástor **Piazzolla** (1921–1992), arr. G. Senanes
Serie del angel (I. 'La muerte del angel') 3:53
Achilles Liarmakopoulos, trombone; Edson Scheid, violin I;
Han Jiyun, violin II; Raul Garcia, viola; Arnold Choi, cello;
Samuel Adams, double bass 8.572596

29 **Trombones Together**
Richard **Wagner** (1813–1883)
Overture to *Tannhäuser* (extract) 0:49
Slovak Philharmonic Orchestra; Michael Halász 8.550136

30 **Tuba Solo**
Ralph **Vaughan Williams** (1872–1958)
Tuba Concerto in F minor (I. Prelude) 4:38
James Gourlay, tuba; Royal Ballet Sinfonia; Gavin Sutherland 8.557754

31 **Tuned Percussion Instruments**
Individual demonstrations 1:18

32 **Untuned Percussion Instruments**
Individual demonstrations 1:31

33 **Percussion Together**
Aram Il'yich **Khachaturian** (1903–1978)
'Sabre Dance' from *Gayane* (extract) 0:28
St. Petersburg State Symphony Orchestra; André Anichanov 8.554054

34 **Saxophone Solo**
Darius **Milhaud** (1892–1974)
Scaramouche for alto saxophone and orchestra (III. 'Brazileira') 2:38
Theodore Kerkezos, saxophone; Philharmonia Orchestra; Martyn Brabbins 8.557063

35 **Harp Solo**
Claude **Debussy** (1862–1918)
Deux Danses (No. 2: 'Danse profane') 4:34
Emmanuel Ceysson, harp; Orchestre National de Lyon; Jun Märkl 8.572675

36 **Piano Solo**
Ernő **Dohnányi** (1877–1960)
Variations on a Nursery Song, Op. 25 (Theme & Variation 1: *Poco più mosso*) 1:37
Eldar Nebolsin, piano; Buffalo Philharmonic Orchestra; JoAnn Falletta 8.572303

37 **Tormod's Favourite Music**
Edvard **Grieg** (1843–1907)
'In the Hall of the Mountain King' from *Peer Gynt* Suite No. 1 2:23
Norrköping Symphony Orchestra; Mats Rondin 8.578203

Total Time: 77:57

That is the end of

My First Orchestra Book

But if you enjoyed it, there are other things you can explore!

My First Orchestra App

Tap any words or pictures and hear the text narrated, extracts of music, animations and sound effects.

My First Classical Music Book

www.naxos.com/naxosbooks/mfcmb

The Carnival of the Animals

With music, narrated verses and animated animals, the carnival has never been so alive!